Sam on the Hill

by Sidney Allen
illustrated by Carolyn Croll

Practice Decodable 6

McGraw Hill Education

Bothell, WA • Chicago, IL • Columbus, OH • New York, NY

MHEonline.com

Send all inquiries to:
McGraw-Hill Education
8787 Orion Place
Columbus, OH 43240

ISBN: 978-0-02-145978-0
MHID: 0-02-145978-9

Printed in China.

8 9 10 11 12 DSS 27 26 25 24 23

I have a  .

dog

The  is Sam.

dog

The  is up, up, up.

hill

Sam is on the  .

bike

I am on the  .

hill

Sam is on the  .

hill